Rhythms of Prayer

C14

Raymond Chapman is Emeritus
Professor of English in the University
of London, and a non-stipendiary
priest in the Diocese of Southwark. He
is a Vice-chairman of the Prayer Book
Society and is the author of literary
and religious titles, including *The
Ruined Tower*, *The Loneliness of Man*,
Intercessions at the Eucharist and *Faith
and Revolt: Studies in the Literary
Influence of the Oxford Movement*.

Rhythms of Prayer

A round-the-year prayer guide

Raymond Chapman

CANTERBURY
PRESS
Norwich

First published in 1997 by The Canterbury Press Norwich
(a publishing imprint of Hymns Ancient & Modern Limited,
a registered charity)
St Mary's Works, St Mary's Plain
Norwich, Norfolk, NR3 3BH

© Raymond Chapman 1997

Raymond Chapman has asserted his right under the
Copyright, Designs and Patents Act, 1988, to be identified
as Author of this Work

British Library Cataloguing in Publication Data

A catalogue record for this book is available
from the British Library

ISBN 1–85311–159–7

*Typeset by David Gregson Associates, Beccles, Suffolk
Printed and bound in Great Britain by
St Edmundsbury Press Ltd, Bury St Edmunds, Suffolk*

Contents

Preface

This is a book for Christians who are leading busy lives, but are not too busy to remember the duty and privilege of prayer. Many such books have been written and valued in past years when life was perhaps not quite so stressful and hurried as it is today. Their devotional attitudes often derived from particular types of church membership and could sometimes become exclusive and even tendentious. One of the happy features of our time is the growing together of Christians in shared respect and willingness to learn from other traditions. It is hoped that the prayers contained here, some derived from traditional forms but mostly newly composed, will help to unite in personal devotion many who are still separated in public worship.

Here are prayers and meditations for Christians who have not developed a practice of systematic prayer, and equally for those who pray regularly but feel the need of some guidance in structuring and extending their devotions. May they be led to deeper prayer and to the study of some of the great masters of the spiritual life. These are essentially personal prayers, using the first person singular except in those intended for church groups. Christians pray in the name of Jesus Christ and this ascription should be added as seems appropriate, perhaps at the end of a period of prayer.

The author is an Anglican priest, with a strong preference for the Book of Common Prayer and the Authorized Version of the Bible, and a liking for the use of the second personal singular in addressing God. It is hoped that none of these preferences have intruded as prejudices. Biblical quotations are from the New Revised Standard Version, or from the Authorized Version for some well-known passages. The forms *you* and *your* are used for God, since this is now the usage familiar to most worshippers. Where the *thou* words occur in quotations or in traditional prayers, they have been retained.

Introduction

Some years ago there was a popular play called *Outward Bound* about a number of people who find themselves on an ocean liner and gradually realize that they are all dead and heading for judgement. One of them, a clergyman, feels inadequate to give the help which he should, and he is urged by an old cockney woman who is of the company to pray. She reminds him, 'There's no harm in habits if they're good habits — and prayer is a good habit.'

How good is our habit of prayer? Are we still stuck in a childish pattern of prayer, repeating the same formulas with a sense that there is Someone up there to be kept happy and propitiated, or getting a vague sense of security and a job done for the day? We are told to receive the Kingdom as little children, but there is a great difference between being childlike and being childish. It is a difference which comes out also in the Greek of the New Testament: Jesus tells his disciples to be like little children, using a neutral word for this stage of life, but St Paul has a different word when he says how on becoming a man he put away childish things. We need to keep the childlike simplicity of perfect faith and trust, but also to be prepared to grow in prayer as we do in other ways.

Prayer is to be a good habit, springing from the best that we can offer of our experience, our intelligence, and above all our love of God. A good habit, but certainly a habit: not in the weak sense of something repetitive that we do not bother to control, but in the strong way of something that becomes so much a part of ourselves that we are incomplete when we neglect it. For this purpose we must set aside time, when it can best be found, but preferably early in the day. Prayers which are not said in the morning tend not to be said at all. There should be a minimum time, not too ambitious at first but gradually increasing. The length of time must be individually decided, perhaps in consultation with a priest or minister, but ten minutes is a realistic minimum, and half an hour is within most people's ability.

Whatever length of time is decided, it should be firmly kept. Does this seem too mechanical, a sort of stopwatch devotion? Without some discipline, prayer tends to be pushed to the margin even by the most devout: there is always something else to do which appears more pressing or more attractive. We find time for other things and we can find time for prayer. There are days when prayer seems less easy and spontaneous, and concentration is harder. The offering of time even when prayer becomes difficult is an act of obedience which is itself an act of faith. We can never gauge the quality of such an offering. The feelings are important, but the will is important too, and is generally more easily controlled.

Prayer also needs some structure, not to be constricting of our spontaneous approach to God, but to give shape and constancy. It is good to begin always with a direction of intention, knowing and acknowledging the presence of God, never absent but now particularly recollected. Adoration follows: praise, awe and love for the whole being of God as he is, unknowable and yet revealed to us. This beginning of prayer lifts us from current anxieties and distractions and concentrates the mind.

For most of the prayer time, it is well to follow where the personal situation leads. There will be thanks for particular benefits and mercies to ourselves and others; admission of sins and prayer to be forgiven; petition, or requests for our desires and needs; intercession for the help of others, known or unknown to us. It is wise not to make rigid divisions for these aspects of prayer within the appointed time. Sometimes we shall linger over one of them as the principal need of the day.

Prayer is not all asking; it is not a shopping list of all the things we should like to have. Yet it is right to ask, to bring our hopes before God and in so doing to test their quality. Does something much desired seem really to be in accordance with the will of God as we understand it? Of course God knows all our needs, and has his purpose for each one of us. But we are encouraged and even commanded to ask, so that our relationship with him includes all aspects of our lives and offers them to be used as he wills. Making intercession for others, we are making ourselves available to be used in God's service if the opportunity is given.

The Lord's Prayer gives us a perfect pattern. It is the supreme prayer of Christians, taught by

Jesus to his disciples in all ages. It begins with direct address to God in majesty, prays for the universal acknowledgement of his holiness and the fulfilment of his purpose. It asks for the supply of bodily needs, forgiveness of sins with commitment to extend the same love to other people, then desire to be spared from further sin and kept safe from all that is evil. It ends with a great ascription of adoration. This wonderful prayer should always be included in our own prayers.

Let us then be ambitious in prayer, but not impatient. All Christians, including the saints and mystics, have known periods, sometimes over many years, when there seems to be no progress. There are times of spiritual dryness when we feel no communication. These are times to hold fast to the discipline of prayer, waiting until we are ready to receive God's calling to new understanding and fresh devotion. Some days seem full of distractions, when we cannot concentrate as we wish. Turn the distractions into prayers, offering the negatives to become positive. A time of prayer spent wholly in recalling the will from distraction, and thus acknowledging our desire for God, is not wasted.

There is much strength in adding to personal prayers a set order such as the offices of Morning and Evening Prayer in the Book of Common Prayer, or other orders used in various churches, and thus joining in spirit with other Christians who are using the same form. In the course of life we may make changes, explore new ways and find what is most effective. Advice from books on prayer, and from people experienced in spiritual direction, may be valuable.

There are many methods and types of prayer, many ideas about place, posture and preparation, and these may be worth exploring as prayer life deepens. Yet let us never forget that we come in prayer to a loving Father, who welcomes us and takes delight in whatever we offer with sincerity. A child does make elaborate preparations before running with requests to a loving parent. Sincerity and complete honesty are essential for prayer.

Prayer is essentially a close relationship with God, as revealed in Jesus Christ. Our growth in prayer should be a deepening of that relationship. We seek, in the words of a familiar prayer, to know him more clearly, love him more dearly, and follow him more nearly. The life of prayer is

a life filled with Christ. If our closest human rela-
tionships do not develop and mature, they tend
to wither away. Surely we cannot be satisfied
with failure to increase our love and understanding in the greatest relationship of all.

It is hoped that the suggestions for prayer
which are offered in this book will help the
formation and progress of personal prayer. Short
orders for prayer in the morning and evening
and during the day can be used alone or as a way
into more extended prayers. Devotions for the
principal times of the Christian year can be
added to give extra prayer at the appropriate
seasons. Meditations are for use when time can
be set aside to reflect more deeply on particular
situations. There are prayers for individual or
corporate use in connection with activities in the
local church. Finally, there is a selection of some
great prayers that have been long used and
loved.

Prayer is the simplest form of speech
That infant lips can try;
Prayer the sublimest strains that reach
The Majesty on high.

J. Montgomery 1771–1854

Daily Prayers

Morning Prayers

To be said as early as possible, before starting the activity of the day.

✱ Early in the morning I will direct my prayer to you.

✱ Dear God, thank you for your love in creating me and in taking care of me all through my life, and especially during the past night. Blessed be your holy name for ever.

✱ O my God, I believe that you are present here; I worship and adore you with all my heart.

✱ In your mercy keep me this day free from sin and safe from danger. Give me grace to know

and perform and accept your holy will at all times. Bless those that I shall meet today, and make me a blessing to them. Keep me from impatience and resentment when difficulties come. Guard and bless those I love, and bring them safely through the day.

* Lord Jesus, I promise today to try to imitate the example of your love, to be like you in patience, humility, purity and care for others. I will try not to give way to those temptations which I know are a danger to me, and to avoid as well as I can all that might draw me away from you.

* Our Father, who art in heaven, hallowed be thy name, thy Kingdom come, thy will be done, on earth as it is in heaven. Give us this day our daily bread. And forgive us our trespasses, as we forgive those who trespass against us. And lead us not into temptation, but deliver us from evil. For thine is the kingdom, the power and the glory, for ever and ever. Amen.

One of these verses from hymns may help to start you on the new day.

* Forth in thy name, O Lord, I go,
  My daily labour to pursue;
  Thee, only thee, resolved to know,
  In all I think or speak or do.

* Only, O Lord, in thy dear love
  Fit us for perfect rest above;
  And help us this and every day
  To live more nearly as we pray.

* Direct, control, suggest this day
  All I design, or do, or say;
  That all my powers, with all their might,
  In thy sole glory may unite.

* When morning gilds the skies,
  My heart awaking cries,
  May Jesus Christ be praised:
  Alike at work and prayer
  To Jesus I repair;
  May Jesus Christ be praised.

PRAYERS DURING THE DAY

St Paul tells the early Christians to 'pray without ceasing' (1 Thessalonians 5:17). This may seem to be an impossible command in an ordinary life, but it is certainly true that our praying should not and need not be confined to set times of concentration. As we come closer to God through prayer and worship, we become aware of his continual presence with us. We speak to him as we do to a human companion who knows us intimately and needs no long explanation of our feelings and needs. These quick prayers are sometimes called 'arrow prayers': they are sent towards their divine target quickly and without the preparation given to longer periods of prayer. They keep us mindful of our dependence on God and our trust in him.

Such prayers are fuelled by the prayers which we offer at more length, in private devotion or in public worship. God never refuses to hear those who call upon him sincerely, but our link with him is made stronger by our considered acts of worship. The good habit of regular prayer enables our arrow prayers to be easy and natural, unforced and offered in confidence.

They can be very brief: often 'Sorry', 'Thank you', 'Help', say all that is needed. We pray too for other

14

people, perhaps strangers whose names we do not know but whose trouble we can see: 'Please help her' — 'Give him peace of mind.' Circumstances may allow a little more, perhaps something of this kind:

✱ O my God, I am very sorry for having sinned against you, and by your help I will not sin again.

✱ Thank you for this new sign of your love and care for me.

✱ Give me the strength and courage that I need.

✱ Keep me firmly in your care.

✱ Let me have the right words for what I have to say.

✱ Guide me to make the right decision now.

The wonderful Jesus Prayer, much used in the Orthodox Churches, can be said and repeated at any time:

* Lord Jesus Christ, Son of God, be merciful to me, a sinner.

It says all that we need. It acknowledges Jesus as the Christ, the Anointed One, true Son of God. It prays for mercy, whether for pardon or for help, directs it towards the individual who prays, and acknowledges the sinfulness which God alone can remove.

The best prayers, as always, will be those made in our own words which are really meaningful to us.

EVENING PRAYERS

To be said at a suitable time when the main activity of the day is over.

* The Lord Almighty grant us a quiet night and a perfect end.

* Dear God, thank you for your love in creating me and in caring for me all my life, and keeping me safe through this day.

Think of any faults that you know you have committed during the day.

* O my God, I am very sorry for having sinned against you. Please forgive me, strengthen me against temptation and lead me in the right way for all my life to come.

* Bless me and keep me through the hours of darkness, bless all those I love, and all whom I find it hard to love. Be near to all who are in trouble or sorrow tonight, remembering particularly … Receive in mercy all who will die before the morning.

* Save us, O Lord, while waking, and guard us while sleeping, that awake we may watch with Christ and asleep we may rest in peace.

As you lie down say:

* I will lay me down in peace and take my rest, for it is you alone, Lord, who makes me dwell in safety.

Some traditional prayers and verses for the end of the day.

✳ Visit, we beseech you Lord, this dwelling, and drive far from it all the snares of the enemy. May the holy angels dwell here to preserve us in peace, and may your blessing be upon us evermore.

✳ Watch, dear Lord, with those who wake, or watch, or weep tonight, and give your angels charge over those who sleep. Tend your sick ones, O Lord Christ. Rest your weary ones. Bless your dying ones. Soothe your suffering ones. Pity your afflicted ones. And all for your love's sake.

✳ O Lord, support us all the day long of this troubled life, until the shades lengthen, and the evening comes, and the busy world is hushed, and the fever of life is over, and our work is done. Then, Lord, in your mercy grant us a safe lodging, a holy rest, and peace at the last, through Jesus Christ our Lord.

✳ Lord Jesus Christ, who at this evening hour lay in the sepulchre, and thereby sanctified the grave to be a bed of hope to your people, make us so to be filled with sorrow for our sins which were the cause of your Passion, that when our bodies lie in the dust our souls may rise with you, who are alive with the Father and the Holy Spirit, ever one God, world without end.

✳ Glory to thee, my God, this night
For all the blessings of the light;
Keep me, O keep me, King of Kings,
Beneath thine own almighty wings.

✳ Round me falls the night,
Saviour, be my light:
Through the hours in darkness shrouded
Let me see thy face unclouded:
Let thy glory shine
In this heart of mine.

✳ Jesus, give the weary
Calm and sweet repose;
With thy tenderest blessing
May our eyelids close.

* The day thou gavest, Lord, is ended,
  The darkness falls at thy behest;
  To thee our morning hymns ascended,
  Thy praise shall sanctify our rest.

For a longer meditation at the end of the day see page 71.

Devotions for Holy Communion

BEFORE COMMUNION

Psalms 84, 85, 86 and 116 verses 10 to the end are suitable.

✱ Blessed be the Lord Jesus Christ on his throne of glory and in the most holy sacrament of the altar.

✱ Lord, I am not worthy to receive you, but only speak the word, and I shall be healed.

✱ Come to my heart, Lord Jesus,
There is room in my heart for thee.

21

❋ Merciful God, do not look at my unworthiness, but accept sorrow for my sins, joy for the love freely given, and thanks for the grace of this holy sacrament.

❋ Through the Body and Blood of my Lord, may I receive new strength for my Christian service.

For a longer meditation see page 57.

AFTER COMMUNION

Psalms 100 and 150 are suitable.

   ❋ Strengthen for service, Lord, the hands
     Which holy things have taken.

❋ Lord, now lettest thou thy servant depart in peace.

❋ I live, but not I, Christ lives in me.

* Thank you, dear Lord, for feeding me with this holy food. Forgive what has been imperfect in my worship, and keep me faithful in the way that lies before me.

* God be praised for this wonderful sacrament of love. May the communion which I have received give me grace to show that praise in all my living.

For a longer meditation see page 58.

SPIRITUAL COMMUNION

When unable to be in the church and receive communion, if possible read some of the preliminary prayers and the readings for the day. Then, joining in love and worship with all who receive the sacrament, say:

* Dear Lord Jesus, since I cannot now receive you through the offering of bread and wine, I pray that you will come to me and fill me with your grace. Come and cleanse me, heal me, strengthen

me in your service, and unite me to yourself now
and for ever.

* Soul of Christ, sanctify me,
   Body of Christ, save me,
   Blood of Christ, invigorate me,
   Water from the side of Christ, wash me,
   Passion of Christ, strengthen me.
   O good Jesus, hear me,
   Within your wounds hide me.
   Do not let me be separated from you.
   From the power of evil defend me,
   In the hour of my death call me,
   And bid me come to you,
   That with your saints I may praise you for
        ever.

Seasonal Prayers

We all experience more than one kind of year. As well as the calendar year starting on 1 January, each birthday makes us aware of a new year of life. As children and students, or if we have children of our own, we know that a new academic year starts in September. The Christian Church keeps its own year, starting in Advent, about the beginning of December. Public worship marks in various ways the life of Jesus Christ on earth, from the promise of his coming to his Passion, Resurrection and Ascension, and the descent of the Holy Spirit, passing into the long season of Sundays after Trinity or after Pentecost, when other themes in the life of the ongoing Church are explored. Into the yearly cycle of weeks beginning each Sunday, there is woven commemoration of the saints.

There is thus a regular yearly reminder of the foundations of our faith. The whole purpose of God is always present and working, but we are limited by time and it is good for us to concentrate on particular aspects. There is also, in psychological terms, wisdom and strength in being aware of the rhythm of each year and its natural seasons which are marked by Christian commemorations. People lose a great deal today by always thinking about the next period of pleasure or relaxation instead of making the most of the routine as well as the special times, and commercial interests encourage this continual living ahead.

The life of devotion is strengthened by additional prayers and reflections at the great times of the church year. A few minutes more each day at these times will build up our awareness of what God has done in Christ.

ADVENT

This season, starting on the fourth Sunday before Christmas, is rich in themes. We remember the expectation of the Messiah often expressed by the Old Testament prophets, and its fulfilment in a more wonderful way by the Incarnation. It has long been customary to reflect at this time on the Four Last

Things: Death, Judgement, Hell and Heaven — seeing our lives and all history in the perspective of eternity. As we think of the coming of Christ born as a human child, we think also of his Second Coming when God's purpose is complete. All these ideas are found in the familiar Advent hymns.

Advent is a penitential season, not so rigorous as Lent, but calling for some extra devotion and perhaps some little act of self-denial. It is not easy to keep a good Advent when the anticipation of Christmas reaches back into November, but we should try. There is no need to refuse every pleasure and celebration, but Christians have always found that the joy of Christmas is increased if they have properly prepared for it.

ADVENT PRAYERS

* The glory of the Lord shall be revealed, and all people shall see it together, for the mouth of the Lord hath spoken (Isaiah 40:5).

* The Holy Spirit will come upon you, and the power of the Most High will overshadow you; therefore the child to be born will be holy; he will be called Son of God (Luke 1:35).

✳ I thank you, loving God:
  For the divine plan of our redemption.
  For the signs given to ancient Israel.
  For the vision of the prophets.
  For the preparation of Mary and Joseph.
  For the message of John the Baptist, the
    forerunner.

✳ Dear Lord Jesus Christ, who for our sakes came to share our human condition, to be born as a helpless infant, to suffer pain and death so that we could be restored to fullness of life, give me grace now to prepare quietly and humbly for your coming, so that I may receive you with my deepest love and hold close to you in faith all my life.

✳ As I enjoy and give thanks for all the blessings of my life, may I remember that I am mortal, and live so that when I die to this world I shall come to you for eternity.

✻ The Lord God comes with might, and his arm rules for him (Isaiah 40:10).

✻ 'Surely I am coming soon.' Amen. Come, Lord Jesus (Revelation 22:20).

CHRISTMAS

This is the most familiar and most enjoyed of all the Christian seasons. Its true meaning seems to be lost for many people in material and sometimes excessive indulgence. Christians must not despise permissible pleasures, which are part of God's bounty to us. A time of relaxation and celebration in the middle of the winter is good for everyone. Let us enjoy Christmas to the full, but keep its wonder always before us, and try to let others know the true reason why we rejoice at this time. The birth of a child is a natural cause for thanksgiving, but this Child is like no other. God takes our human nature and brings us into a new and restored relationship with himself. The bitter end of the life of Jesus on earth lies ahead, but the Incarnation itself is the beginning of our redemption.

CHRISTMAS PRAYERS

* Unto us a child is born, unto us a son is given, and the government shall be upon his shoulder. And his name shall be called Wonderful Counsellor, the Mighty God, the Everlasting Father, the Prince of Peace (Isaiah 9:6).

* To you is born this day in the city of David, a Saviour, which is Christ the Lord (Luke 2:11).

* Thank you, dear God, for all the joys of Christmas, for our human love and friendship, for the pleasures which we take together. As I enjoy them, let me always remember that all good things come from you, and keep me thankful also for the deep truth of this season. Thank you for the birth that brought new life for me and all the human race.

* May I know in my heart, and share with others, the simple joy of the shepherds, the praise of the angels, the love of the Holy Family.

✳ May the holy Child of Bethlehem, true God and true Man, be close to me this day and every day.

✳ Peace on earth and mercy mild
God and sinners reconciled.

✳ For you who revere my name the sun of righteousness shall rise, with healing in his wings (Malachi 4:2).

✳ The Word became flesh and lived among us, and we have seen his glory, the glory as of a father's only son, full of grace and truth (John 1:14).

EPIPHANY

Christmas does not end on Christmas Day or Boxing Day. The season is kept for twelve days until the Feast of the Epiphany on 6 January, the celebration of the visit of the Wise Men to Bethlehem, as told by St Matthew. They were from outside Judea, and were the first non-Jews to see the infant Christ. We thank God for revealing himself in his Son to the whole world. In the star which led the Wise Men to Bethlehem we see the light of God leading us to himself, and in the gifts which they offered we are taught to make our own offerings of the best that we have.

Epiphany Prayers

❋ Arise, shine; for thy light is come, and the glory of the Lord is risen upon thee (Isaiah 60:1).

❋ We have seen his star in the east, and are come to worship him (Matthew 2:2).

❋ Almighty God, as you led the Wise Men to your Son by the light of a star, give me your light to lead me always to him, never turning aside from the true way.

❋ In the gift of gold, I give thanks for the Kingship of Christ, Lord over all the world.

In the gift of frankincense, I give thanks for the high priesthood of Christ, Lord over his Church.

In the gift of myrrh, I give thanks for the saving death and resurrection of Christ, Lord over time and eternity.

✳ Blessed are you, Lord of all, for revealing yourself to me in Jesus Christ. Give me wisdom to know your will, give me humility to kneel before you in worship, give me generosity to share the great love that you give to me.

✳ Nations shall come to your light, and kings to the brightness of your dawn (Isaiah 60:3).

✳ By the tender mercy of our God, the dawn from on high will break upon us (Luke 1:78).

LENT

Lent, which begins forty days before Easter, is the season in which we think of the many hardships and privations which Jesus suffered during his years on earth. We reflect particularly on the forty days in the wilderness when, alone and fasting, he experienced and overcame temptation. We pray at this time for strength to resist temptation, to overcome our sins and to grow in knowledge and love of God. Lent is generally thought of as a time of 'self-denial'. It is indeed good to have some rule of abstaining from a permissible pleasure, in order to strengthen the will and to make a practical token of our penitence and desire to do better. More important is the resolve to make this season a time of extra prayer and devotion, with closer study of the Bible and other spiritual reading.

LENT PRAYERS

* Rend your hearts, not your clothing. Return to the Lord your God (Joel 2:13).

* Resist the devil and he will flee from you (James 4:7).

* Jesus, as you fasted forty days in the wilderness, give me strength in my resolve to deny myself for your sake.

✳ Jesus, as you lived there, exposed and lonely, give me patience in the disappointments and discomforts of this life.

✳ Jesus, as you resisted temptation and drove away the tempter, give me grace to resist temptation, and shield me from the power of evil.

✳ Now, Lord, guide me seriously to think of my many sins, of the wrongs I have done and the good that I have failed to do. Take away my self-love and give me true repentance for all the ways in which I have offended against you. Show me especially the sins to which I am most liable, and open my heart to your defence against them. As I repent of my sins, let me not dwell upon them but let me fully accept the pardon which you give to all who truly trust in you.

✳ May this Lent be for me a time of growth in faith and hope and love, turning regret to new resolve, and sorrow to new joy.

✱ Do not enter into judgement with your servant, for no one living is righteous before you (Psalms 143:2).

✱ If we confess our sins, he who is faithful and just will forgive our sins and cleanse us from all unrighteousness (1 John 1:9).

For meditations on temptation and penitence see pages 60 and 61.

PASSIONTIDE

The last two weeks of Lent are traditionally known as Passiontide. The rule and devotions of Lent are continued, but Christians direct their repentance more closely towards the last sufferings of Jesus and his death on the Cross. It is a time of giving thanks for his sacrificial love, and of sorrow for failure to respond to it. We try in imagination to follow the events of his last days and especially those of Good Friday.

PASSIONTIDE PRAYERS

* He is despised and rejected of men; a man of sorrows, and acquainted with grief (Isaiah 53:3).

* Christ also suffered for you, leaving you an example, so that you should follow his steps (1 Peter 2:21).

* Jesus, despised and rejected for me: accept my love and sorrow.

Jesus, betrayed by a trusted follower: accept my love and sorrow.

Jesus, facing the hour of death in the garden: accept my love and sorrow.

Jesus, deserted by every friend: accept my love and sorrow.

Jesus, denied by one greatly loved: accept my love and sorrow.

Jesus, mocked and alone among enemies: accept my love and sorrow.

Jesus, cruelly flogged for no offence: accept my love and sorrow.

Jesus, crowned with piercing thorns: accept my love and sorrow.

Jesus, carrying the crushing weight of the Cross: accept my love and sorrow.

Jesus, in thirst and rending pain: accept my love and sorrow.

Jesus, feeling the last desolation: accept my love and sorrow.

Jesus, divine in the hour of mortal death: accept my love and sorrow.

Jesus, a broken body in a borrowed tomb: accept my love and sorrow.

* Lord Jesus Christ, you forgave to the uttermost those who caused you to die. Forgive me now and always for my sins, for my part in the human sin which brought you to your Passion. Give me the inward sight to face, as far as mortal understanding may, the dreadful reality of the Cross, and also to accept its assurance of divine love. May the power of the Cross be my shield from all evil in this life, my comfort at the hour of my death, and my way to eternal life.

* God forbid that I should glory save in the cross of our Lord Jesus Christ (Galatians 6:14).

✳ God so loved the world, that he gave his only Son, so that everyone who believes in him may not perish, but may have eternal life (John 3:16).

EASTER

Easter is the supreme Christian festival, the celebration of the Resurrection which is the crown of our faith. It speaks to us of the power which overcomes death, and gives assurance of eternal life to all who trust in the saving love shown in Jesus Christ. God has given the only remedy for the sin which brought death into the world, and humanity is restored. We learn to see signs of the Resurrection in the many instances of renewal and fresh hope in our lives.

EASTER PRAYERS

✳ After two days he will revive us; on the third day he will raise us up, that we may live before him (Hosea 6:2).

✳ Christ has been raised from the dead, the first fruits of those who have died (1 Corinthians 15:20).

✳ Alleluia. Wonderful, loving Lord, thank you for this season, the yearly assurance of what I know is always true. Nothing can separate me from the love which overcame death. May I live as one who lives always in the presence of the Risen Christ, revealing him in all I say and do. In this world, and in all that lies beyond it, my hope is only in him. Alleluia.

✳ Teach and enable me to see the fruits of the Resurrection all around me. In the spring of every year, in recovery from sickness of body or mind, in times of reconciliation, in all fresh enterprises offered in his name, I shall give thanks that all is made new in Jesus Christ. May I discern the hope of renewal through him even in the desolate places where hope seems lost, and may I have the grace to bring others out of darkness into his marvellous light.

✻ Lord Jesus, as you were known to the disciples at Emmaus in the breaking of bread, come to me in the holy communion of your body and blood. With your divine life, cleanse me, heal me, strengthen me, unite me to yourself for ever.

✻ I have told the glad news of deliverance in the great congregation (Psalms 40:9).

✻ I am the resurrection and the life: he that believeth in me, though he were dead, yet shall he live: and whosoever liveth and believeth in me shall never die (John 11:25,26).

✻ Christ is risen: he is risen indeed. Alleluia.

ASCENSION

Forty days after his Resurrection, Jesus returned to heaven from which he had come to live and die as man. This is a great and wonderful mystery, revealed to the disciples in an act of his being lifted up out of their sight. He completed the teaching which he had been giving them in the previous weeks by commanding them to go out and spread the Good News to all people. Our human nature is taken up into the presence of God through his body, now risen and glorified.

ASCENSIONTIDE PRAYERS

❋ God has gone up with a shout, the Lord with the sound of a trumpet (Psalms 47:5).

❋ While he was blessing them, he withdrew from them and was carried up into heaven (Luke 24:51).

❋ Lift me up, Lord God, free me from all that holds me back from you, raise me in heart and mind to a new assurance of your love, drawing my weak human nature into your divine perfection. Thank you for the peace that passes all understanding.

❋ Lord Jesus Christ, as you commanded your disciples to teach all nations, give me grace to be a minister of the Gospel wherever it is your will to lead me. May my words speak of you, the Lord who has ascended from earth but is always present, my hands be ready in your service, my feet swift to go where you call me.

✽ As I rejoice through faith in the Ascension of my Lord, may his grace fill me with desire to live as he wants me to live in this world, neglecting no duty, refusing no gift of his love, ready at the end to be raised to the heavenly place where he has gone before.

✽ The Lord says to my lord, sit at my right hand (Psalms 110:1).

✽ He who descended is the same one who ascended far above the heavens, so that he might fill all things (Ephesians 4:10).

PENTECOST

Pentecost — or by its traditional English name, Whitsunday — comes fifty days after Easter. (It is from the Greek word for 'fifty'.) Now we celebrate the coming of the Holy Spirit on the Apostles, appearing like tongues of fire and giving them the power to tell of the good news in many languages. This is sometimes regarded as 'the birthday of the Church'. From that time, the Holy Spirit is continually present with all believers, bringing strength and encouragement, and leading them, as Jesus had promised, into the truth.

PENTECOST PRAYERS

* I will put my spirit within you, and make you follow my statutes (Ezekiel 36:27).

* All of them were filled with the Holy Spirit and began to speak in other languages, as the Spirit gave them ability (Acts 2).

  * Come, Holy Ghost, our souls inspire
    And lighten with celestial fire;
    Thou the anointing spirit art,
    Who dost thy sevenfold gifts impart.

✱ Gracious Spirit, Holy Spirit of God, fill me with faith and hope and love so that I may take my part in the divine purpose and be more worthy of my calling to follow Christ.

✱ As the Apostles brought the Gospel to many people, so grant me power to speak of the faith which I know, with tact and discernment, with wisdom and compassion, so that others may come to the knowledge of your saving love.

✱ May the Holy Spirit give me right judgement in all things, guide me into the way of truth, strengthen me against temptation and bring me after this life into the perfect knowledge and love of God.

✱ When you send forth your spirit they are created; and you renew the face of the ground (Psalms 104:30).

✱ We know that he abides in us, by the Spirit that he has given us (1 John 3:24).

TRINITY SUNDAY

On the Sunday after Pentecost we praise the Holy Trinity, God the Father, Son and Holy Spirit. This is the greatest of Christian mysteries and we cannot fully understand it with our limited minds while we are in this world. We need to know only that this has been the faith of Christians from the earliest years of the Church. It has been a continual defence against corruption of that faith and the errors of those who claim new revelations beyond the word of God revealed in Jesus Christ and holy scripture. It is always associated with the highest praise and adoration, a celebration of God's majesty, greatness and power.

TRINITY PRAYERS

* Holy, holy, holy is the Lord of Hosts; the whole earth is full of his glory (Isaiah 6:3).

* Blessing, and honour, and glory, and power, be unto him that sitteth upon the throne, and unto the Lamb for ever and ever (Revelation 5:13).

✳ And now, Holy Spirit,
  Teach us to know the Father, Son,
  And thee of both to be but one.
  That through the ages all along
  This may be our endless song:

  Praise to thy eternal merit,
  Father, Son and Holy Spirit.

✳ Almighty God, on this day I desire only to offer my praise for all that you are. Beyond my furthest understanding, infinite in power and majesty, you have revealed yourself to me in Jesus Christ. I am not worthy to raise my eyes to your glory, yet I know that you are close to me in my weakness and failures, in my sorrows and my joys, in the beauty of the world, in human friendship and love. Thank you.

✳ Now, in the months to come, keep before me all that I have learned in considering the life of Christ from his first coming to his Ascension and the gift of the Holy Spirit. May I follow in his steps, guided by his example and empowered by his Spirit, and daily praising God, Unity in Trinity.

❋ I praise you, O God, I acknowledge you to be the Lord. Glory be to God on high.

❋ The glory of the Lord shall be revealed, and all flesh shall see it together (Isaiah 40:5).

❋ Let us continually offer a sacrifice of praise to God, that is, the fruit of lips that confess his name (Hebrews 13:15).

SAINTS' DAYS

So many Christians have been considered worthy of special remembrance that it is possible to find a saint for almost every day of the year. We all perhaps have some favourite saint whose life for God seems to speak to our own and give us encouragement. Special services are widely used for the Apostles, Evangelists, John the Baptist, St Michael and all angels, and often for others specially associated with a church or a place. A saint is not just a 'good' person, but one whose life was closely conformed to the will of God and who witnessed for him to the world, sometimes by martyrdom. Remembering the saints, we are reminded that the Church exists not only on earth — the Church Militant — but much more fully in the company of all faithful Christians who have died — the Church Triumphant.

PRAYERS FOR SAINTS' DAYS

❋ He leadeth me in the paths of righteousness for his name's sake (Psalms 23:3).

❋ These are they which came out of great tribulation, and have washed their robes, and made them white in the blood of the Lamb (Revelation 7:14).

❋ I thank you, my God, for the example of all the saints, especially for (N) who is commemorated today. May I too follow closely in the steps of Jesus Christ, so that my life shall give to the world whatever kind of witness you require for me. Grant me, unworthy but trusting in your constant love, eternal life with all your blessed ones.

* The whole Church, living and departed, praises you, O God. Accept my praise and prayer, feeble and inadequate in words but offered in faith. Lift up my thoughts, to be blended with the harmony of heaven.

* For all the saints who from their labours rest,
Who thee by faith before the world confessed,
Thy name, O Jesu, be for ever blessed,
Alleluia.

* Their kingdom shall be an everlasting kingdom (Daniel 7:27).

* Be perfect, therefore, as your heavenly Father is perfect (Matthew 5:48).

THE VIRGIN MARY

Mary was chosen to be the mother of Jesus, to give human life to the Son of God. We know from the gospels the beauty of her life, from her humble acceptance of the message by the angel of the Annunciation to her sorrow at the Cross and her presence with the Apostles after the Ascension. Then she passes from recorded history, but Christians in all ages have delighted to honour her, especially on days associated with some point in her life.

PRAYERS FOR MARY'S FESTIVALS

✳ The King's daughter is all glorious within: her clothing is of wrought gold (Psalms 45:13).

✳ He hath regarded the low estate of his handmaiden: for, behold, from henceforth all generations shall call me blessed (Luke 1:48).

✳ May the faith of Mary, told by the angel that she would bear the Son of God, be my example.
May the family love of Mary, visiting her cousin Elisabeth also with child, be my example.

May the humility of Mary, giving birth in the squalor of a stable, be my example.

May the patience of Mary, driven into a strange land to save her child from death, be my example.

May the perseverance of Mary, seeking long for her son and finding him in the Temple, be my example.

May the maternal love of Mary through years of growth and learning, be my example.

May the constancy of Mary, close to her Son in his death, be my example.

May the fellowship of Mary, in company with the Apostles as the Church was built, be my example.

* Dear God, as you gave grace to the blessed Virgin Mary, your chosen one, to be the mother of Jesus, give to me and to all your people the grace that we need to live according to your will.

* Look with mercy on all women who suffer hurt and injustice, for themselves or for those they love. May the love of Mary reach out to them and to their oppressors, to draw all people into the way of peace.

✻ Who can find a virtuous woman? For her price is far above rubies (Proverbs 31:10).

✻ Standing near the Cross of Jesus was his mother, and his mother's sister, Mary the wife of Clopas, and Mary Magdalene (John 19:25).

Grace Before Meals

To give thanks before a meal is one of the best practices of regular prayer. Times of eating give focal points in the activities of the day and an opportunity for natural recollection of God's goodness. In giving thanks for the food which we need to maintain life, we recall also the other blessings which we have received. Grace is a simple form of family prayer but can, and should, equally be said by a Christian eating alone. A simple, 'Thank you, God' can mean a great deal if it is said with sincerity and recollection. Some of the following graces may be found helpful.

* For what we are about to receive, may the Lord make us truly thankful.

* Bless, Lord, this food to our use and us in your service.

✳ God give us grateful hearts, and make us mindful of the needs of others.

✳ For these and all your mercies, we give you thanks, O God.

✳ Thank you, Lord, for this food and for all your goodness to us.

✳ May God bless us in this meal, and in all our lives together.

✳ Thanks be to God for life, and for food to sustain it.

✳ May God, present with us here, bless the food which he has given.

✳ Blessed be you, O Lord, bringing food from the earth.

✳ The eyes of all wait upon you, O Lord, and you give them food in due season.

Meditations

These are passages to aid personal reflection and to turn it to prayer. It is suggested that the meditation be read slowly and followed by silent consideration from which spontaneous prayer may come. If a particular idea seems helpful, pause and think about it, letting it lead you as God wills. You may continue the meditation or leave it there for that occasion: this section is offered solely as a way of focusing devotion, not of directing it. In each case, the thought is drawn towards some aspect of the life of Jesus, our pattern and support in our own Christian lives.

If this method is found useful, apply it to Bible reading, taking a passage and letting it guide you into prayer and resolution.

BEFORE COMMUNION

✳ I am coming to receive this sacrament,
  but I do not know fully what I am doing.
  Wise men have thought and prayed about it
  and been no nearer to explaining what
      happens.
  It is enough to know that Jesus told us what to
      do:
  as the centurion says to his servant 'Go' and he
      goes,
  so my Lord says, 'Do this' and I do it.
  The disciples at supper must have wondered
      what he meant,
  but they had learned to trust him in all things.
  I do want this to be a good communion,
  but there may be inattention, wandering
      thoughts, impatience.
  He gave the bread and the cup to those who
      were unworthy of them,
  who did not love him as much as they
      professed,
  who immediately afterwards deserted and
      betrayed him.
  Perhaps they remembered when they were
      broken and in hiding,

that he had said it was for the remission of sins.
Thank you, I accept the invitation to a meal for
   sinners.

AFTER COMMUNION

✸ I am so thankful for what I have received
   that I want to join my little thanks with the
       Church's prayer,
   the great thanksgiving, the Eucharist.
   I still know that I am not worthy
   but I have obeyed the command,
   I have offered my will to serve where my desire
       was too weak,
   I have shared in the work of the whole Church,
   I have been joined to the source of her life,
   and I have been brought very close to people I
       scarcely know.
   who were guests with me at God's table.
   Lord, please help me to find you in the ordi-
       nary meals,
   and in all the simple things of life,
   because bread and wine are simple but
       wonderful.
   When lepers came to Jesus for healing,

they found they were cleansed as they went on
    their way:
make me clean now,
as I go on my way from this holy sacrament.

SUNDAY EVENING

✱ The weekend has passed very quickly, time of
    rest and recreation,
time for myself and my own affairs.
There has been worship, closer time with God,
and the encounter with his word, his special
    word for me.
I should like to go on enjoying leisure,
Not meeting the demands of other people.
If I love the Church,
I must remember that it is not a private club,
but a concentration of power and love for the
    whole world.
I have had the chance of being among my
    fellow Christians,
and some are a joy and pleasure to know.
Others are not so nice or amusing as some
    weekday people
who seem to believe in nothing.
Jesus died for everyone,

not just for the believing ones, not just for the
amusing ones.
Jesus often liked to go apart, to be alone or with
a few friends,
away from the pressure of people wanting his
help,
but he always came back, to heal and to teach,
to love until the end.
Once when he came down from the mountain
of Transfiguration —
and his friend Peter had wanted to stay there
for ever —
he was met by a distressed father, with a boy
terribly afflicted.
Tomorrow someone in trouble may need me.

TEMPTATION

* This is an attractive possibility.
I know it would be wrong, and yet —
there would be no great harm, nobody hurt,
just a little pleasure, a little advantage.
At least there can be nothing wrong in thinking
about it,
so long as I don't allow it to go too far.
Yet something will not let me alone

with my pleasant thoughts of what might be:
this distant warning system called my con-
    science
tells me to stop here, listen to no evil.
Jesus, cruelly tempted in the wilderness,
did not listen or stop to consider
but told the tempter to go right away.
Lord, deliver me from evil.

PENITENCE

* Saying 'sorry' is easy,
Feeling sorry is not too difficult,
really caring is very much harder.
Lord, make me understand that being truly
    sorry for sin
is not being embarrassed by my own silliness,
not being troubled that my image of myself has
    had a knock,
not even feeling upset by knowing how bad
    some things are.
I have hurt you by sin,
by returning disobedience for your glorious
    freedom,
self-love for your unlimited love.
It is not my own image that is damaged —

it is your image in me, the face of Christ
wrenched with pain that I have caused him.
Lord Jesus, when you walked among us,
you came to sinners right where they were,
knew what was turning them from God and
    brought them home.
I know you are as close to me now as you were
    to them.
Take my 'sorry', fill up all that it lacks,
and send me on my way again to do better.

IN TIME OF TROUBLE

* In bad times like this
    I have always been told to think of others who
        are worse off,
    and remember how Job was patient in
        suffering:
    but this is not Job's trouble; it is all mine.
    Lord, it is hard to think much of other people,
    but because this trouble is mine, it is also yours.
    Perhaps being hurt and empty, with nothing
        but pain to offer,
    is what faith means.
    Jesus loved those who came to him in their
        emptiness,

and on the Cross he was totally emptied and
    helpless.
He said, 'Take up your cross,' and it is heavy,
but always in church there is the cross,
and before he went to the Cross he said, 'Thy
    will be done.'
It is hard for me to say it, but he said it also for
    me.
Lord, accept my need and bring me through
to where I can again think of the needs of others
with a deeper understanding than before.
After the Cross there was life:
please, bring from this point of death, a resur-
    rection.

THANKSGIVING

* Today I just want to say, Thank you.
My prayers are usually full of requests
because I come to you as my Father, the loving
    giver,
but today I just want to say, Thank you.
My prayers are usually full of anxiety and
    regret
because I come to you as my Father, the
    pardoner,

but today I just want to say, Thank you.
So many things, big and small, given in your
    love,
but this is not the time to try to name them all,
because I can accept the wonderful truth of
    being loved.
Jesus gave thanks to his Father,
making the bread and wine his most precious
    gift for ever:
so, with all who share his bounty,
I just want to say, Thank you.

FAMILY AND FRIENDS

* Lord, thank you for other people,
for those who make my life whole and mean-
    ingful,
who give me purpose, share my happiness,
and are always there when things go wrong.
Thank you for giving me this little vision
of your infinite love for all your creation.
Through joy in the fullness of being human,
may I come closer to the beauty of holiness.
Jesus lived with family, walked with friends,
knew the disappointments as well as the joys
but never limited or closed his love.

Lord, thank you for other people,
even the ones who are difficult for me to love.
Help me to share your love for them.

FAMILY PROBLEMS

∗ This hits too hard.
The family is where I always come for support
  and comfort
when the big world is too much to bear.
Now when I reach out in pain towards that
  assurance,
there seems to be nothing to touch, nothing to
  hold.
When words fail, there is only pain and silence
because where we love most will always hurt
  most.
Saint Paul gave a lot of advice to Christian
  families,
most of which is really not very helpful in this
  situation,
except in telling us that trouble is nothing new.
When human arms are slack, draw me into the
  arms of God.
His human family must give him a great deal of
  trouble.

Jesus caused grief to his family, who did not
understand,
and his Mother stood in silence to watch him
die,
so we are together in the knowledge of love
that gives pain.
Please help us to hold together through this
time.
We are a very small part of your big family
but so important to us — please mend it.

In Doubt and Despair

* It is like being in a dark place
where nothing is certain, nothing familiar.
Things that were firm and secure now fall away
from me,
words that gave strength no longer call them
back.
My fear is not some real trouble threatening
but the fear that there is nothing, no meaning.
Where are you now, God in whom I trusted,
in this desert of my uncertainty?
When the feeling and the desire are weak,
God, take my will to trust and to believe.
Jesus knew temptation in the wilderness,

anguish in the garden of betrayal,
desolation on the Cross when all power had
      gone.
If God could feel forsaken by God,
I can hold fast in this darkness,
knowing that it cannot for ever resist the light.

ANGER

✳ Lord, I am very angry,
I feel wronged, insulted, badly used.
When I try to put it aside, turn to other
      thoughts,
still the dark rage shakes me.
My mind tells me that this is a little, meagre
      thing
against the great wrongs people suffer daily;
my conscience tells me that this is a sinful
      feeling,
no part of one who claims to follow Christ.
But nothing moves the poison creeping within
      me,
controlling what I think, prompting what I will
      do.
Lord, heal this sickness, restore love that has
      vanished.

Jesus showed his anger against the ungodly
but never hated, never refused his unbounded
     love;
and for those who betrayed him, hurt him,
     killed him,
he had only words of healing and pardon.
I forgive those who trespass against me —
please, God, forgive me.

SUFFERING OF THE WORLD

✻ God, where are you, where are your promises?
There is so much suffering —
little sorrows, heavy burdens, ultimate misery
which makes no sense of a world created in
     love.
Every day, every hour, I hear of some new
     distress —
sickness, war, violence, homelessness,
the obscenity of children abused and killed.
If I cry in accusation, demanding to know why,
take my doubt, and turn it to a prayer.
Let not the evil things make me forget the good.
Let not the great horrors close my eyes
to the trouble near me, needing my help.
Above all, keep me close to Jesus on the Cross,

bringing human pain into divinity
in a mystery of compassion that silences ques-
    tions.
We can take this world of pain with the Cross,
    or without it;
please keep me faithful when I do not under-
    stand.

BEFORE A JOURNEY

* As I go on my way, hold me in your care
safe from harm and free from sin.
I shall meet many people for a short time,
and some may make me feel impatient,
and some will find me irritating —
Lord, help me to travel with love and consider-
    ation.
Please be my guide in new places,
my light when the way forward seems un-
    certain.
Bless my home and those I love,
watch between us while we are apart,
and bring me back when journeying is
    done.
Jesus travelled many miles, often weary and in
    danger,

always healing, teaching, pardoning people as
he passed by.
Lord, make this journey part of my pilgrimage
to you;
as I go on my way, cleanse me and make me
whole.

CHRISTIAN UNITY

* I don't always like my own church
but it suits me well enough not to change it,
and I believe it is the right place for me to
worship.
Others go to their own places
and I wish them well, but seldom think about
them.
What seems strange to me may be right for
them,
and there is no way of containing all that you
are.
We are all your children, equal in love:
we ought to know one another better.
Please help me to accept that people are
different,
have different needs, different ways of finding
you,

70

and to come closer to other Christians
in the little ways that will lead to greater.
Jesus prayed that we should all be one.
Make me part of that prayer
in the time and the way of your own purpose.

GOING TO BED

∗ Now at the day's end
I thank you, God, for all your love has given,
for care and protection, work done, people
     known;
and regret for my poor response to love,
for opportunities lost, good words unsaid,
moments of hostility to some who have passed
     my way.
Another day between the mysteries of birth
     and death —
let me learn from it, make the next day
     better.
Jesus, sleeping peacefully in a storm on the
     lake,
let me rest now, secure in your love,
for the darkness reveals your peace, as the light
     your glory.
Jesus, sleepless in the garden of agony,

have mercy on those for whom the night is
    darkness indeed —
who suffer pain, anxiety, unhealed sin,
those who are without a bed, a home.
May I remember in the morning, the compas-
    sion of the night.

Church Group Prayers

The worship which is the heart of church life is helped by much voluntary work, some closely connected with the services and some dealing with buildings or outside activities. All are vital to the good order of the church and are to be offered with reverence. The Bible often reminds us that we have many different gifts, all acceptable to God. The officiating priest or minister says a prayer in the vestry before a service. Those who come together as a group, or who offer individual talents, may also wish to dedicate their work with a short prayer.

BELLRINGERS

(1) PRACTICE

∗ We give thanks for our fellowship and the pleasure we share. May we remember the

holiness of this place, and in all we do and say be
worthy of our calling and show our thankfulness
for the privilege of ringing together.

(2) Service Ringing

* As we come together again for the call to
worship, we pray that the sound of these bells
may proclaim your glory, summon the faithful,
speak to the indifferent, and make your people
ready for your service.

(3) Weddings

* Bless, we pray, the couple for whose wedding
we are about to ring, and grant them continuing
love in their life together. May the sound of these
bells be a signal of joy for them, and for all who
are present with them today.

CATERING GROUP

* May God who cares for both body and spirit bless our work, and use our skill in his service so that those who share in the food we offer may share also in the fellowship of Christian love.

CHOIR

* We give thanks for the divine gift of music and song, praying that we may use it to the praise and glory of the giver, to express our own devotion and to beautify the worship offered here.

CHURCH CLEANING

* Bless, O Lord, our task of making this church clean and fit for worship. May its brightness be a witness to your glory and an aid to the reverence of those who enter here. Take our hands, and use them in your service.

CHURCHYARD AND GARDEN

✱ Almighty God, eternally present in the beauty of nature, and with whom the souls of the faithful departed are at peace, bless our work in caring for all that lies around our church, that it may be a fitting approach to the worship within.

FINANCE COMMITTEE

✱ Lord, give us wisdom to be good stewards of that which is entrusted to us. Guard us from being anxious for the future or irresponsible in our present concerns. Make us remember that all things come from you, and that we are called to this service for the welfare of the Church and the good of your Kingdom.

FLOWER ARRANGING

✱ Lord, you have given the beauty of flowers to your creation. Please give us skill now to make your house lovely and pleasant in your sight, and in the sight of those who are to worship here.

INTERCESSOR

✸ Lord, speak through my lips, to ask on behalf of the congregation those things which are needful for them and pleasing in your sight. Make me fluent in speech but not loving my own invention, brief in words but not abrupt in utterance. Make me an instrument of the worship which we offer together.

LESSON READING

✸ Lord, as you have revealed yourself to us through the Bible, to guide us into the way of truth, be with me now in making your word known through my lips. Give me grace to play my part in our worship, reading clearly, reverently and to your glory.

SERVERS

✸ Lord, as we come to the service of the altar, we give thanks for the privilege of assisting in the celebration of this holy sacrament. Guide us in our duties, keep us from anxiety about the lesser things, and give us true reverence that we may receive the grace of your presence here.

SIDESMEN

✳ Lord, you have called us to help in the worship of your church. Teach us to discern the needs of all who come for worship, to encourage the diffident, reassure the anxious, have a cheerful word for the downcast, and respect the silence of those who like to be left alone. When any task distracts us from devotion, fill our emptiness with your grace.

SUNDAY SCHOOL TEACHERS

✳ Dear Lord, lover and protector of children, use us in your service to bring these little ones closer to you. Make us wise in our teaching and patient in our response, to prepare the way for their fuller knowledge and service in the years to come.

VISITING

✳ Go with us, Lord, into the homes of your people. Give us wisdom in speaking and wisdom in hearing, to bring comfort to the distressed, peace to the troubled, patience to the unquiet, and love to all whom we shall meet.

A PRAYER FOR GENERAL NEEDS

✳ Loving God, bless this parish [*church, fellowship*] to serve you faithfully in all ways. As you have called us to worship together, strengthen us to support each other, to make your love known by word and example, and to know ourselves part of the company of all Christian people. Pardon and correct all that is wrong among us, accept and increase what is good, and unite us in the grace of our Lord Jesus Christ, the love of the Father and the fellowship of the Holy Spirit.

Traditional Prayers

Here are some prayers which have been used and loved by many. They have expressed devotion through centuries of the Christian faith, and in many church allegiances. Browse through them, find any which speak particularly to your nature or to your immediate need, and use them within your own times of prayer. Sometimes one of these prayers will give scope for meditation, reflecting silently on the truths which it expresses. You may be led on to explore other writings by some of these Christian men and women, whose prayers are set down here in the order of their lives.

> Christ be with me, Christ within me,
> Christ behind me, Christ before me.
> Christ beside me, Christ to win me,
> Christ to comfort and restore me.
> Christ beneath me, Christ above me,
> Christ in quiet, Christ in danger.

Christ in hearts of all who love me,
Christ in mouth of friend and stranger.

St Patrick *c.* 389–461

Thanks be to thee,
O Lord Jesus Christ,
for all the benefits which thou hast given me;
for all the pains and insults which thou hast
    borne for me.
O most merciful Redeemer, friend and
    brother,
may I know thee more clearly,
love thee more dearly,
and follow thee more nearly,
for thine own sake.

St Richard of Chichester 1197–1253

God, of thy goodness, give me thyself,
for thou art sufficient for me.
I may not ask for anything less
than what befits my full worship of thee.
If I were to ask anything less I should
    always be in want,
for in thee alone do I have all.

Julian of Norwich 1342–*c.* 1416

Teach me, dear Lord, to serve thee as thou
    deservest,
to give and not to count the cost,
to fight and not to heed the wounds,
to toil and not to seek for rest,
to labour and not to ask for any reward
save that of knowing that I do thy will.

                Ignatius Loyola 1491–1556

Govern all by thy wisdom, O Lord,
so that my soul may always be serving thee
    as thou dost will,
and not as I may choose.
Do not punish me, I beseech thee,
by granting that which I wish or ask,
if it offends thy love, which would always
    live in me.
Let me die to myself that so I may serve
    thee;
let me live to thee, who in thyself art the
    true life.

                St Teresa of Avila 1515–82

O blessed Jesus, give me stillness of soul in
    thee.
Let thy mighty calmness rule in me.
Rule me, O though King of gentleness, King
    of peace.
Give me control, great power of self control,
Control over my thoughts, words, actions
From all irritability, want of meekness, want
    of gentleness,
Dear Lord deliver me.
By thine own deep patience,
give me patience, stillness of soul in thee.
Make me in this and in all, more and more
    like thee.

St John of the Cross 1542–91

Lord Jesus,
I give thee my hands to do thy work.
I give thee my feet to go thy way.
I give thee my eyes to see as thou seest.
I give thee my tongue to speak thy words.
I give thee my mind that thou mayest think
    in me.
I give thee my spirit that thou mayest pray
    in me.

Above all, I give thee my heart
that thou mayest love in me thy Father and
    all mankind.
I give thee my whole self that thou mayest
    grow in me,
so that it is thee, Lord Jesus, who lives and
    works and prays in me.

Lancelot Andrewes 1555–1626

O my God,
since thou art with me,
and I must now, in obedience to thy
    commands,
apply my mind to these outward things,
I beseech thee to grant me the grace to
    continue in thy presence;
and to this end do thou prosper me with thy
    assistance, receive
all my work, and possess all my affections.

Brother Lawrence 1611–91

O God, in whom nothing can live but as it
    lives in love,
grant me the spirit of love,

which does not want to be rewarded,
    honoured or esteemed,
but only to become the blessing and
    happiness of everything that wants it;
love which is the very joy of life,
and thine own goodness and truth within
    the soul;
who thyself art Love, and by love our
    Redeemer,
from eternity to eternity.

William Law 1686–1761

Almighty God, the giver of all good
    things,
without whose help all labour is
    ineffectual,
and without whose grace all wisdom folly,
grant, I beseech thee, that in all my
    undertakings
thy Holy Spirit may not be withheld from
    me:
but that I may promote thy glory,
and the salvation both of myself and of
    others.

Samuel Johnson 1709–84

Deliver me, O God, from a slothful mind,
from all lukewarmness, and all dejection of
    spirit.
I know these cannot but deaden my love to
    thee;
mercifully free my heart from them,
and give me a lively, zealous, active and
    cheerful spirit;
that I may vigorously perform whatever
    thou commandest,
thankfully suffer whatever thou choosest for
    me,
and be ever ardent to obey in all things thy
    holy love.

John Wesley 1703–91

Teach me, dear Lord,
frequently and attentively to consider this
    truth:
that if I gain the whole world and lose thee,
in the end I have lost everything;
whereas if I lose the world and gain thee,
in the end I have lost nothing.

John Henry Newman 1801–90

O Lord, in whom is my hope, remove far
    from me, I pray thee,
all empty hope and presumptuous
    confidence.
Make my heart so right with thy most holy
    and loving heart,
that hoping in thee I may do good;
until that day when faith and hope shall be
    abolished by sight and possession,
and love shall be all in all.

                    Christina Rossetti 1830–94

O my Saviour,
let me not fall by little and little,
or think myself able to bear the indulgence
    of any known sin
because it seems so insignificant.
Keep me from sinful beginnings,
lest they lead me on to sorrowful endings.

                    Charles Spurgeon 1834–92

Now unto him that is able to do exceeding abundantly above all that we ask and think, according to the power that worketh in us, unto him be glory in the Church by Christ Jesus throughout all ages, world without end. Amen. (Ephesians 3:20–21).